BULLIES

Caitie McAneney

PowerKiDS press™

New York

Published in 2015 by The Rosen Publishing Group, Inc.
29 East 21st Street, New York, NY 10010

First Edition

Editor: Caitie McAneney
Book Design: Mickey Harmon

Photo Credits: Cover (series logo) Alhovik/Shutterstock.com; cover (banner) moham'ed/Shutterstock.com; cover (image), p. 11 Twin Design/Shutterstock.com; p. 5 Dawn Shearer-Simonetti/Shutterstock.com; pp. 7, 15, 19, 21 Monkey Business Images/Shutterstock.com; p. 9 Pavel L Photo and Video/Shutterstock.com; p. 13 funstock/Thinkstock.com; p. 16 Anna Omelchenko/Shutterstock.com; p. 17 Jasper Cole/Blend Images/Getty Images; p. 22 Sergey Novikov/Shutterstock.com.

Library of Congress Cataloging-in-Publication Data

McAneney, Caitlin.
  Bullies / Caitie McAneney.
      pages cm. — (Let's talk about it)
  Includes index.
  ISBN 978-1-4777-5785-7 (pbk.)
  ISBN 978-1-4777-5786-4 (6 pack)
  ISBN 978-1-4777-5784-0 (library binding)
  1. Bullying. I. Title.
  BF637.B85M297 2015
  302.34'3—dc23
                              2014024182

Manufactured in the United States of America

CPSIA Compliance Information: Batch #CW15PK: For Further Information contact Rosen Publishing, New York, New York at 1-800-237-9932

CONTENTS

WHAT IS BULLYING?

Have you ever **witnessed** bullying? Bullying is when a person tries to hurt someone else. Bullies try to make themselves feel powerful by making others feel weak.

Bullying can happen anywhere—on the school bus, in the hallways at school, and at the park. Bullying at school can make it hard to learn and play. Bullying at home or in your neighborhood can make it hard to feel safe and be yourself. Luckily, there are ways to make your school and community into bully-free **zones**.

Many times, bullying happens when adults aren't paying attention. It's important to tell adults when you witness bullying.

KINDS OF BULLYING

Bullies hurt people in many ways. They might call someone a mean name or **threaten** to hurt them. This is meant to hurt the **victim's** feelings. Other times, bullies hurt victims **physically**. They might hit, push, or kick someone. Some bullies trip people or steal their things.

TELL ME MORE

Bullying even happens on the Internet. A bully could post lies and hurtful comments about a person so everyone can see. That's called cyberbullying.

Did you know that leaving someone out is a kind of bullying? A bully might tell other people not to be friends with someone. They might spread lies about the person to make them feel bad.

Some people bully others about their height, weight, hair color, or how smart they are. It hurts the other person's feelings.

WHO IS INVOLVED?

Bullying may seem like a problem that's just between the bully and the victim, but other people play a part in bullying, too.

Bullies often surround themselves with friends who will help pick on a victim. They might spread lies or keep teasing the victim. Others laugh or clap when a bully is hurting someone. These people allow the bully's hurtful actions to continue and make things even worse. The best part to play is the defender, or someone who speaks up for the victim.

TELL ME MORE

Bystanders are people who witness bullying happening, but don't try to stop it. Bystanders have the power to be defenders if they stand up for the victim!

Have you even been the defender in a bullying situation? You can be a defender by telling a teacher about bullying, speaking up for the victim, or comforting the victim.

9

WHY DO PEOPLE BULLY?

Bullies pick on others for many reasons. They might live in a home where teasing and hurting others is normal. Older siblings or adults might pick on them, so they think bullying is okay. Some bullies feel bad about themselves, and hurting others makes them feel powerful.

Having power makes a bully feel popular. Every time someone bullies, they get attention from the people around them and the victim. Bullying could be the only way that person knows how to get attention.

Bullies can be boys or girls, big or small. Even if a bully seems big and mean, they might feel small and weak on the inside.

TELL ME MORE

Bullies might think picking on someone will win them friends. Some people are afraid to not be the bully's friend.

WHY ME?

Have you ever been the victim of bullying? You might wonder why bullies chose you to pick on. The answer isn't always clear.

Sometimes bullies pick on others for no reason. It might not make any sense. Bullies sometimes pick on people who are different from them. They probably can't understand or don't care why someone might look or live differently. Sometimes bullies pick on kids who are smaller or kids who can't stick up for themselves. This makes the bully feel more powerful.

Bullies often choose victims who get very upset.
When bullies make someone mad or sad, it gives
them a feeling of control.

WHAT HAPPENS?

What happens when bullies pick on people for a long time? The victims might start to feel very bad about themselves. They could have low **self-esteem** as they grow up. Victims might have a hard time paying attention in school. People might become afraid to show who they really are or what they really like to do. A bullying **environment** becomes a place of fear.

TELL ME MORE

Bullies lose attention when people stop listening to them. Over time, people might get sick of their mean words and actions.

What about the bully? Over time, the bully might lose their friends. Many longtime bullies end up in trouble.

An environment with a lot of bullying isn't healthy. There are ways you can step up and make your school or park a healthier place to learn and play.

STOPPING A BULLY

What should you do if a bully starts picking on you? The first step is simple—avoid them. Walk away. Bullies might leave you alone once you're not around. You can avoid bullies by walking a different way in the hallway or sitting away from them.

TELL ME MORE

To grow your self-esteem, you can join a new club or sport. This can help you feel good about yourself as you make new friends.

Sometimes you may need to stand up for yourself. Try to be brave. Tell the bully "no" or "stop." Don't let it show if you get upset because bullies want you to get upset. Pretend their words don't hurt you.

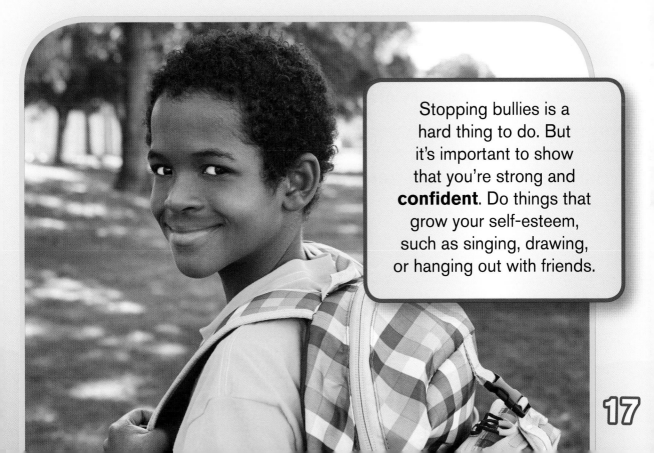

Stopping bullies is a hard thing to do. But it's important to show that you're strong and **confident**. Do things that grow your self-esteem, such as singing, drawing, or hanging out with friends.

STAND TOGETHER

Bullies often pick on people who are walking or sitting alone. If you're being picked on, try to walk or sit with a friend. If you see someone else being bullied, offer to stand by them. Being a friend to a victim can make them feel better. It can also get the bully to stay away.

The more people are on the side of the victim, the harder it is for the bully to hurt them. This will make you a defender and a good person!

If you see a victim who is always bullied, try to get a group of people to stand up for them and be their friends. This will show bullies that the person has a team behind them. It also shows the victim that not everyone is a bully or a bystander.

TELL SOMEONE

Sometimes, a bully is so mean and powerful that you need an adult to stop them. Teachers want their school to be a safe place for learning. If you tell a teacher about bullying, they will likely try to stop it. They might talk to the bully, give warnings, or **punish** the bully for hurting others.

If you're being bullied in your neighborhood, tell your parents. Don't feel **embarrassed** if the bullies get in trouble. They need to know their actions have **consequences**.

TELL ME MORE

Your bullies might be your siblings, other family members, friends, or even coaches. No matter who it is, you should tell an adult if you're being bullied.

You might be scared to tell a teacher you're being bullied or if you see someone being bullied. However, it's the first step to making a safer environment.

GET INVOLVED

Bullying is a big deal. It happens in almost every school and community. We know that bullying can hurt victims and the people around them. Luckily, there are many ways to stop it.

Be a defender, not a bystander. You can create a movement in your school against bullying. Form a team of friends who stand up for others and tell adults when bullying happens. Most of all, be nice to everyone. Friendship and caring are the best ways to stop bullies in their tracks.

GLOSSARY

confident: Having belief in oneself.

consequence: An effect of an action.

embarrassed: Feeling shame or uneasiness.

environment: Everything that is around a living thing.

physically: Having to do with the body.

punish: To make someone pay for a wrong they have committed.

self-esteem: Happiness with oneself.

threaten: To act as though you are planning to hurt someone.

victim: A person who is harmed.

witness: To watch an action or event.

zone: An area.

INDEX

WEBSITES

Due to the changing nature of Internet links, PowerKids Press has developed an online list of websites related to the subject of this book. This site is updated regularly. Please use this link to access the list: www.powerkidslinks.com/ltai/bull